DOMINOES

Five Canterbury Tales

OXFORD
UNIVERSITY PRESS

Great Clarendon Street, Oxford OX2 6DP

Oxford University Press is a department of the University of Oxford.
It furthers the University's objective of excellence in research, scholarship,
and education by publishing worldwide in

Oxford New York

Auckland Cape Town Dar es Salaam Hong Kong Karachi
Kuala Lumpur Madrid Melbourne Mexico City Nairobi
New Delhi Shanghai Taipei Toronto

With offices in

Argentina Austria Brazil Chile Czech Republic France Greece
Guatemala Hungary Italy Japan Poland Portugal Singapore
South Korea Switzerland Thailand Turkey Ukraine Vietnam

OXFORD and OXFORD ENGLISH are registered trade marks of
Oxford University Press in the UK and in certain other countries

This edition © Oxford University Press 2010

The moral rights of the author have been asserted

Database right Oxford University Press (maker)

First published in Dominoes 2008

2016 2015

15 14 13 12

ISBN: 978 0 19 424758 0 BOOK
ISBN: 978 0 19 424722 1 BOOK AND MULTIROM PACK
MULTIROM NOT AVAILABLE SEPARATELY

Printed in China

This book is printed on paper from certified and well-managed sources.

ACKNOWLEDGEMENTS

Illustrations by: Natalia Demidova/PiArt, Moscow

The publisher would like to thank the following for permission to reproduce photographs:

Cover: Bridgeman Art Library Ltd (Chaucer, the Knight and the Squire from 'The Pardoner's
Prologue' of 'The Canterbury Tales', Mileham, Harry (1873-1957) / Private Collection)

Alamy Images pp iv (The Parthenon, Athens/Art Kowalsky), iv (Roman Baths, Bath/David
Ball), iv (Southwark Bridge/Ace Stock Limited), 20 (Araglan Castle/Jon Arnold Images Ltd),
42 (Canterbury Cathedral/Earl Clendennen), 42 (Edward the Black Prince statue, Leeds/
Frederick Fearn), 43 (Alhambra Palace/JLImages), 43 (Court of Lions, The Alhambra/
Travelshots.com), 44 (Makkah, Saudi Arabia/ArkReligion.com); Aquarius Library pp 40
(A Knight's Tale 2001/Columbia), 41 (Heath Ledger, A Knight's Tale/Columbia); Kobal
Collection p41 (Shannyn Sossamon, A Knight's Tale 2001/Columbia/E.Endrenyi); Mary
Evans Picture Library pp iv (Pavia: La Certosa, Italy 1886), iv (All Souls, Oxford 1821/Michael
Rooker, engraved Joseph Skelton), iv (The Franklin, woodcut circa 1500.); OUP pp iv (Houses
of Parliament/Image Source), 38 (coast/Digital Vision), 44 (Machu Picchu/Photodisc);
PunchStock p 44 (Amritsar Golden Temple/Brand X Pictures); Robert Harding Picture
Library p iv (Brittany/Guy Thouvenin); Robert Harding Picture Library p iv (Canterbury
Cathedral/John Miller).

DOMINOES

Series Editors: Bill Bowler and Sue Parminter

Five Canterbury Tales

Geoffrey Chaucer

Text adaptation by Bill Bowler

Illustrated by Natalia Demidova

Geoffrey Chaucer was born in 1343. His father was a rich wine merchant and his mother owned twenty-four London shops. At fourteen he left home to work as a page – or young servant – in the house of a rich woman, the Countess of Ulster. In later life, Chaucer worked for the English king. He was with the English army in France in the 1360s and made two visits to Italy for the king in the 1370s. In his free time he wrote stories and poetry, and he sometimes read these aloud to friends, but his writings did not appear as books until some years after his death in 1400. His 'Canterbury Tales' is one of the most famous pieces of early English literature.

OXFORD
UNIVERSITY PRESS

BEFORE READING

**1 Find out about Geoffrey Chaucer's life.
Circle the correct information.**

a He was born in *1343 / 1743*.

b His parents *were / weren't* rich.

c He left home when he was *14 / 40*.

d He travelled to *America / Italy* a number of times for work.

e He wrote his stories in *Latin / English*.

f He *was / wasn't* a very famous writer when he was alive.

2 Match each photo of a place in *Five Canterbury Tales* with a sentence.

a Athens

b Bath

c Brittany

d Canterbury

e the Thames

f Southwark

g Pavia

h Oxford

1 It's a city in the south-east of England, with a famous cathedral. ☐

2 It's a town in the north of Italy. ☐

3 It's the capital of Greece. ☐

4 It's a city in the south-west of England, famous for its waters. ☐

5 It's part of south London. ☐

6 It's the river that runs through London. ☐

7 It's part of the north-east of France. ☐

8 It's a famous old city for students to the west of London. ☐

CHAPTER ONE
AT THE INN IN LONDON

When March finishes, the rains in April bring the first flowers of spring. At this time the sun is warm and, in England, lots of people go to Canterbury, to the **tomb** of **Saint** Thomas Becket. There they thank the Saint for his past help when they were ill.

My name's Geoffrey Chaucer. It was 16th April 1386, and I was in London at an **Inn** in Southwark, south of the river Thames. I was there with twenty-nine more people. We wanted to go to Canterbury the next day. But before I say more, I want to tell you about some of the people with me.

tomb where people put a dead person

saint a very good person

inn an old name for a hotel where you can eat, drink or stay

First there was a **Knight**. He was a good man, and he **fought** well. He was never afraid. He knew many different countries and was famous in all of them. He always spoke nicely, and he never did any bad things. He was a true friend to everyone, and always helped people when they needed it. His **clothes** were old, dark, and dirty from many years of fighting.

Then there was a **Merchant** with a dark **beard**, and rich red and yellow clothes. He had an expensive hat on his head and good shoes on his feet. 'I'm doing very well,' he always said. He talked about ships and the sea a lot. He was interested in changing money from different countries and was a very quick thinker. He looked richer than he truly was.

Next to the Merchant there was a **Clerk** from Oxford. He was a student and he loved reading books. He had **sad** eyes, and he looked **thin** and hungry. His coat was old and thin, too. He wasn't very good at finding work. When his friends gave him money, he thanked **God** for their help and went at once to the shops for more books. He didn't speak much, but he always said the right thing. He loved learning, and teaching too.

knight someone from a good old family

fight (past **fought**) to hit someone again and again; when someone hits people again and again

clothes people wear these

merchant a person who buys and sells things

beard the hair on a man's face

clerk an old word for someone who works for the church

sad not happy

thin not fat

God an important being who never dies and who decides what happens in the world

2

After the Clerk came a **Franklin** with a white beard and a red, happy face. He liked eating and drinking and having a good time. He asked people from near and far to visit him at home. Summer or winter, his table was always ready for them with lots of good things to eat on it. He was an important man, he knew right from wrong, and people listened to him.

There was a woman from Bath, too. Everyone called her 'The Wife of Bath'. Her face was open, and nice-looking, but she couldn't hear very well. In her red dress, she was a big woman with a big smile, big teeth, and a big red hat on her head. She laughed a lot and talked easily, and she knew all about love.

So there we were, all thirty of us, at the Inn. We all sat down at the table, and the **landlord,** a tall fat man, brought us the best dinner in London. After we finished eating, the landlord smiled, and said: 'We're going to Canterbury tomorrow, and that's four days from here. One by one, let's all tell a story on the road. When you listen to a story, the time goes quicker. And to the teller of the best story we can give a free dinner here at my inn when we get back. What do you say?'

We all said 'yes' happily to the Landlord. The question now was: *Who goes first?*

franklin an old word for someone who doesn't come from an old important family, but who now has money and a big house

landlord a man who has an inn

READING CHECK

1 Choose the correct words to complete the sentences about the story.

a It's ~~spring~~ summer autumn.

b Geoffery Chaucer is in Canterbury London Oxford.

c He's with two friends thirty people his wife.

d They're waiting to go to Canterbury London Oxford.

e The landlord wants all the people to finish eating tell a story have a free dinner.

2 What are the people in the story like? Match two phrases with each picture.

a the Knight ☐ ☐

b the Merchant ☐ ☐

c the Clerk ☐ ☐

d the Franklin ☐ ☐

e the Wife of Bath ☐ ☐

1 always helps people	6 laughs and talks a lot
2 asks a lot of people to his house	7 loves eating and drinking
3 can't hear very well	8 reads a lot
4 hasn't got much money	9 talks about ships and the sea
5 is a good person	10 wears expensive clothes

WORD WORK

Complete the sentences with the correct form of the words on the table.

Labels on image: tomb, beard, clothes, sad, fight, inn, landlord, saint, thin

a Chaucer and his friends are going to visit the ....tomb..... of a ....

b They're staying for a night at an .... before they leave for Canterbury.

c The Clerk doesn't look happy; he's got .... eyes.

d The Merchant and the Franklin both have .... on their faces.

e The Wife of Bath's .... are all red.

f Two knights are .... in this picture.

g He's a .... man, he doesn't eat much, and he's always hungry.

h The .... at the Inn gave them a good dinner.

GUESS WHAT

**The Knight tells the first story. It begins in Greece a long time ago.
Which three things do you think happen in the story?**

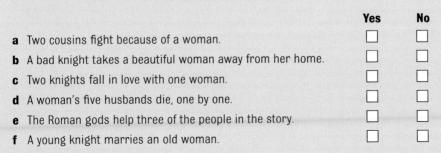

		Yes	No
a	Two cousins fight because of a woman.	☐	☐
b	A bad knight takes a beautiful woman away from her home.	☐	☐
c	Two knights fall in love with one woman.	☐	☐
d	A woman's five husbands die, one by one.	☐	☐
e	The Roman gods help three of the people in the story.	☐	☐
f	A young knight marries an old woman.	☐	☐

5

CHAPTER TWO
THE KNIGHT'S TALE

In the end, the Knight spoke first. 'I'm not very good at this,' he said. 'But I have a wonderful, old story to tell. It's all about love and **war** between men and women, two friends, and different countries – but it's very long. So I'm going to tell you only the most important things. I'm not going take a lot of time answering all those little questions: *What clothes did they wear? What did they eat? How did they fight?* and *Was the weather good or bad?* But let's begin. Are you all ready?' We all said, 'Yes!' at once – and he began to tell his story happily:

war fighting between countries or people

duke the most important man in a big old town

win (*past* **won**) to be the best in a fight

marry to make someone your husband or wife

queen the most important woman in a country

city (*plural* **cities**) a big and important town

king the most important man in a country, or an old town

bury to put a dead body under the ground

enemy someone who is not your friend

Long ago in Greece, **Duke** Theseus fought to make Athens bigger. For many years he made war with different people. One of these wars was with the Amazons. These women were very good fighters, and not afraid of Theseus or the people of Athens. When Theseus **won** the war, he **married** the Amazon **Queen**, Hippolyta. After that, he wanted to take his wife, and her sister, Emely, to Athens.

On the road, they came to the **city** of Thebes. There they saw lots of women with their heads in their hands.

'Why are you crying?' asked Theseus.

'Our city fought a war with Creon,' the women told him. 'He took the city. Now he's **King** of Thebes. And we can't **bury** the dead bodies of our husbands, fathers, and sons, because they were Creon's **enemies**.'

Then Theseus told his wife and her sister, 'You must go to Athens without me. I must fight Creon before I come home.'

So Hippolyta and Emely went to Athens, and Duke Theseus fought Creon. In the end, Theseus killed him. When he was dead, the women of Thebes could bury their men.

In the war, Theseus's men **hurt** two of Creon's knights. Later they brought these two men to the Duke. Their names were Arcite and Palamon. They were **cousins** and good friends. Because they were good fighters the Duke didn't kill them.

'You're coming with me to Athens,' he said. 'There you must live in **prison**. And in the end, you must die in prison too, because you were friends of King Creon – and he was my enemy.'

So Arcite and Palamon went with Theseus to Athens, and for many months they lived in a prison next to the Duke's **castle**.

One day, when Palamon sat by the window, he saw beautiful Emely in the castle garden. He **fell in love** with her at once and cried, 'Oh help! I'm hurt!'

hurt (*past* **hurt**) to do something bad to someone; feeling bad

cousin the son (or daughter) of your father's (or mother's) brother (or sister)

prison a place where people must stay when they do something wrong

castle a big old building; a rich person lives here

fall in love with (*past* **fell**) to begin to love someone

7

'Are you ill, Palamon?' asked Arcite from his bed.

'No, I'm not. But come and look through the window,' answered Palamon.

Arcite looked through the window. When he saw Emely, he fell in love with her, too.

'Emely!' called Hippolyta from the castle. 'Come here. I need you!'

'I'm coming, sister,' answered Emely, and she went at once.

'What a beautiful girl!' cried Arcite. 'She's Queen Hippolyta's sister, Emely, and I love her!'

'You can't love her,' said Palamon angrily. 'I saw her and fell in love with her first – so I'm her lover, not you.'

'Cousin,' answered Arcite, 'Emely doesn't know us, and we're never going to meet her. So I can love her too, I think, and you can't stop me.'

become (*past* **became**) to begin to be

The two cousins, once the best of friends, now **became** the worst of enemies.

Some time later, Duke Perotheus visited Athens. He was Theseus's friend and Arcite's friend too.

'Theseus,' said Perotheus when they met, 'Can Arcite go back to Thebes with me?'

'Of course,' answered Theseus, 'But he must never come back to Athens, or I'm going to kill him.'

Arcite left prison and Athens very sadly. He was very angry about Palamon.

'I'm never going to see Emely again, but Palamon is going to see her from his prison window every day.'

Back in Thebes, Arcite was ill for a long time with love for Emely. When, after many months, he was well again and could leave his bed, his face was thinner and he had a beard. 'I'm very different to look at,' he thought. 'No one is going to know me in Athens now.' So he changed his name to Philostrate, changed his clothes, and went back to Athens.

There he went at once to Theseus's castle, and soon became the Duke's good friend.

All this time Palamon stayed in prison and watched Emely through his window every day. But one night, soon after Arcite was back in Athens, Palamon **climbed** out of the prison window and ran to a **forest** near the castle.

The next day, Arcite went for a walk in the forest. He saw nobody near him, so he spoke freely. But behind a tree Palamon listened carefully.

'Every day Palamon watches Emely far away through his prison window,' began Arcite, 'And, some months ago, I too nearly died of love for her. But now I can meet her and speak with her in the castle when I want. These days

climb to go up or down, or through something using your hands and feet

forest a place with lots of trees

9

I have a new beard, and I'm thinner than I was. So no one here knows me. That's good! Because now I can be Philostrate, and Duke Theseus's good friend. And before I was only his enemy, Arcite.'

Suddenly Palamon came out from behind his tree.

'Fight me, Arcite, you dog!' he cried angrily.

And the two cousins fought.

Just then, Duke Theseus arrived with some knights. Hippolyta and Emely came after them.

'What's all this noise? Philostrate, my friend, why are you fighting?'

Palamon told the Duke everything.

'So, you are my old enemy Arcite!' said Theseus angrily. 'Arcite, Palamon, the two of you must die for this!'

But Emely and Hippolyta cried, 'Please don't kill them!'

So the Duke said to the cousins, 'Very well. I'm not going to kill you. You're free to leave Athens now, but you must come back in a year's time. Arcite, bring with you a hundred knights, and, Palamon you bring a hundred knights, too. There's going to be a big fight between you, and the winner can marry Emely.

So Arcite and Palamon **promised** to come back with their knights, and left Athens.

Theseus began to make everything in the city ready for the big fight. Soon there were new buildings everywhere, and the people of Athens felt excited. 'We're going to have a good time next year,' they thought 'with lots to eat, and lots of drinking and singing – and all because Arcite and Palamon and their knights are coming. It's wonderful.'

After a year, Arcite and Palamon came back to Athens with their best knights. They were ready to fight for Emely.

The night before the fight, Palamon asked Venus for help. '**Goddess** of love, help me to marry Emely,' he said.

At the same time, Emely asked Diana for help. 'Goddess of women without husbands,' she said, 'I don't want to marry. So stop this fight between Arcite and Palamon. But perhaps you can't do that. So then help me to marry well. Which of these two knights loves me more? I want him for my husband.'

That evening Arcite asked Mars for help. 'God of war, help me to win the fight,' he said.

In Olympus, the home of the gods, Diana spoke angrily with Venus and Mars.

'What can we do?' she said. 'Palamon, Emely, and Arcite all want different things. They can't all be happy in the end.'

'The answer's easy,' said the old god Saturn. 'Palamon can win Emely, and Arcite can win the fight. Listen to me. What's going to happen tomorrow is this. . . .'

Back in Athens, it was the day of the big fight. Before things began, Duke Theseus spoke to Arcite, Palamon, and all their knights.

'When a Knight is hurt,' he said to them, 'He must leave the fight. Do you understand?'

'Yes,' said Arcite and Palamon. Then the fight began.

After some time, Palamon was badly hurt, and his men took him away.

Arcite was happy when he saw Palamon go. He stayed on his horse, put his hands over his head, and cried to the people of Athens, 'I'm the winner!'

The people of the city cried back excitedly, 'Arcite's the winner! Arcite's the winner!' When Arcite's horse heard all this noise, it became afraid. Suddenly it stood up on its back legs, and Arcite fell from its back and was badly hurt. Doctors ran to him, but they couldn't help him, and so he died.

In the end, Palamon married Emely, and the two of them buried Arcite very sadly.

Duke Theseus was excited about the **wedding** between Palamon and Emely.

'This is an important day for Athens and Thebes,' he said on their wedding day.

Palamon loved Emely and she loved him, and they were husband and wife for many long and happy years.

wedding the day when two people marry

13

ACTIVITIES

READING CHECK

**Put these sentences in the correct order to tell the Knight's story.
Number them 1–10.**

a ☐ Emely and Palamon marry.

b ☐ Theseus fights the King of Thebes, Creon.

c ☐ Theseus and the women see Arcite and Palamon fighting.

d ☐ Arcite and Palamon fall in love with Emely.

e ☐ Theseus marries the Queen of the Amazons.

f ☐ Arcite wins the fight but he dies.

g ☐ Arcite begins hating Palamon, and Palamon hates Arcite.

h ☐ Theseus puts Arcite and Palamon in prison in Athens.

i ☐ Theseus tells Arcite and Palamon, 'Come back to Athens
and fight in a year's time.'

j ☐ Arcite leaves prison in Athens with a friend.

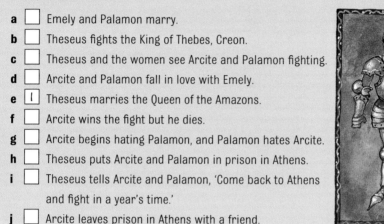

WORD WORK

1 Use the pictures to complete the crossword.

Across

Down

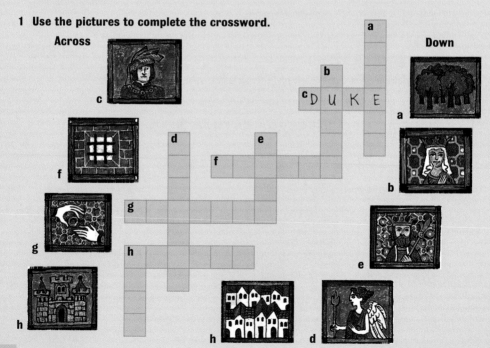

c D U K E

14

2 Complete Palamon's letter to a friend.

Dear friend,

I'm writing to you from Athens. Why? It's a long story.
After the war of Thebes, Creon b_____. The women of
Thebes wanted to b_____ their dead men, but Creon said, 'No!'
Then Theseus fought Creon and w___. His knights h_____ Arcite
and me, and Theseus took us to prison in Athens.

I saw Emely from our prison window, but Arcite f_____
with her too. And so my c_____ and I became e_____.

Theseus was very angry when I c_____ out of prison and
fought Arcite in the forest. We p_____ him to come back
to Athens with one hundred knights. Now it's a year later
and I'm going to fight Arcite. The winner can m_____ Emely.

Your friend,
Palamon

GUESS WHAT

**The Wife of Bath tells the next story. Look at the picture from
the beginning of the story. What happens in the story?**

a It's about . . .

   1 King Arthur and Queen Guinevere.

   2 a sad Italian king and his daughter.

   3 one of King Arthur's knights and a woman.

b What happens to the man?

   1 A beautiful young woman falls in love with him.

   2 He falls in love with a woman from a bad family.

   3 Queen Guinevere asks him a difficult question.

c How does the story end?

   1 The man marries an old woman, but they are happy.

   2 The beautiful woman falls in love with a different knight.

   3 The man marries the young woman, but they aren't in love.

CHAPTER THREE
THE WIFE OF BATH'S TALE

Now it was time for the Wife of Bath's story But before she began, she told us all about her five past husbands. 'My rich old husbands were the best,' she said. 'They did everything for me. Women are more important than their husbands, after all.' Some pilgrims laughed openly when they heard about all her different past lovers, young and old. But when she began her story, we all listened interestedly.

In King Arthur's time, the king and his knights lived in the castle of Camelot. One of Arthur's knights –Tarquin – loved Lucretia, a beautiful young woman with long black hair. But she didn't love him. One day she sat under a tree by the river, when suddenly Tarquin **rode** his horse out of the forest and took her in his arms.

'Help!' cried Lucretia, but Tarquin carried her away quickly on his horse to an old house on a hill far from Camelot. There he put her in a dark room and closed the door behind her.

At once, King Arthur called his knights to him. 'Find Tarquin and Lucretia,' he said, 'and bring them to me.'

They soon brought Tarquin and Lucretia to the king. He was angry with Tarquin. 'When a knight from Camelot **treats** a woman badly, he must die,' said Arthur.

But Queen Guinevere felt sorry for Tarquin. So she asked her husband, 'Can I give a different **punishment** to him?'

ride (*past* **rode**) to go on a horse

treat to do something to someone with good or bad feelings

punishment when you do something bad to someone after they do something bad to you

'Of course,' said the king.

Then she said to Tarquin, 'Tell me the answer to this important question: what do women want most of all?'

Tarquin didn't know. So he said nothing.

Then the queen said, 'Tarquin, you can leave Camelot now, but you must come back in a year with a good answer to my question, or you die.'

So Tarquin went from village to village and town to town. And always he asked different women Guinevere's question.

In one village they answered, 'We want money.'

In the next village they said, 'We want to be happy.'

In one town, they told Tarquin, 'We want to hear nice things from our lovers.'

Days became weeks, and weeks became months. Soon it was time for Tarquin to go back to Camelot. He felt bad because he didn't have a good answer to Guinevere's question.

On the road to Camelot, Tarquin rode his horse through a forest. It was dark and not easy to see there. After some time, he got off his horse and began to walk. Just then, he saw twenty-four beautiful young women in front of him. They were all in green dresses, and they sang beautifully, laughed, and moved in and out of the trees. But when Tarquin came near, they suddenly left – and the only thing there in front of him was an **ugly** old woman.

Tarquin told his story to her, and asked her Guinevere's question.

'I can tell you the answer,' she said. 'But first you must promise me something.'

'What?' asked Tarquin.

'You must **pay** me **back** later for my help.'

'Of course, old woman,' laughed Tarquin.

In Camelot, Tarquin went at once to the queen.

'What do women want most of all?' asked Guinevere,

'To **rule** their husbands,' answered Tarquin.

Guinevere asked the women in the room, 'Is that right?'

'Yes,' they all said.

'Tarquin, you're a free man,' said Guinevere,

Just then, the ugly old woman from the forest came into the room.

'Wait!' she cried. 'That young man's answer came from me!'

'It's true,' said Tarquin.

'And now you must pay me back,' said the old woman.

ugly not beautiful

pay back (*past paid*) to do something good or give money to someone after they do something good to you

rule to tell someone or the people in a country what they must or mustn't do

'How much money do you want?' asked Tarquin.

'I don't want money,' she said. 'You must marry me!'

So Tarquin married the old woman that afternoon. That night, before they went to bed, his new wife was sad.

'What's the matter, husband?' she asked. 'Why don't you look at me?'

'Wife,' he said. 'I feel ill when I see your face.'

'But my ugly face is a good thing,' she answered. 'No man is going to want to take me to bed, and so I'm always going to be **faithful** to you. What do you want – a quiet, faithful but ugly wife, or a beautiful but not faithful wife?'

'I don't know,' said Tarquin. 'You **choose** for me.'

When she heard this, the old woman felt happy. She now ruled her husband.

'**Kiss** me,' she said. 'I'm going to be your faithful *and* beautiful wife.'

So Tarquin kissed the ugly old woman, and at once she became young and beautiful.

And after that, Tarquin lived very happily with his beautiful, faithful wife for many years.

faithful true to your husband or wife and not having lovers

choose (*past* **chose**) to think which thing, of a number of things, you want

kiss to touch lovingly with your mouth

READING CHECK

Correct the mistakes in these sentences.

a Lucretia ~~is~~ *isn't* in love with Tarquin.

b Tarquin takes Lucretia to a castle far away from Camelot.

c King Arthur feels sorry for Tarquin.

d Queen Guinevere asks Tarquin a question about men.

e Twenty-four young women tell him the answer to the question.

f Tarquin comes back to Camelot after a week with the answer to the question.

g Tarquin marries the old woman because he is in love with her.

h The old woman is happy because she loves her husband.

i When Tarquin marries her, she becomes young and beautiful.

WORD WORK

1 Find seven more words from *The Wife of Bath's Tale* in the wordsquare.

D	A	T	R	E	A	T	I	N	P
I	P	A	I	K	N	B	T	O	F
G	A	S	D	I	H	E	R	T	A
E	R	T	E	S	C	Y	E	N	I
P	U	N	I	S	H	M	E	N	T
R	L	G	R	A	O	E	S	S	H
I	E	E	L	T	O	U	H	E	F
Q	U	F	R	Y	S	T	U	A	U
T	C	R	O	U	E	P	A	L	L

2 Use the correct form of the words from Activity 1 to complete the sentences.

a Guinevere is a loving and ..faithful.. wife to King Arthur.

b King Arthur was a good king and .... England for many years.

c When Tarquin .... his wife, he doesn't become ugly.

d Guinevere's .... for Tarquin is to answer a question.

e King Arthur wants to kill Tarquin because he .... Lucretia badly earlier.

f The old woman in the forest is very ....

g The Wife of Bath .... to tell a story about a knight perhaps because the Knight's story is about two knights.

h Tarquin .... his horse from village to village and asks women everywhere his question.

GUESS WHAT

The Clerk of Oxford tells the next story about a husband and wife. Tick the boxes.

		Yes	No
a	The husband . . .		
1	isn't faithful to his wife.	☐	☐
2	is an Italian king.	☐	☐
3	does some very bad things to his wife.	☐	☐

		Yes	No
b	The wife . . .		
1	always wants to please her husband.	☐	☐
2	is from a rich family.	☐	☐
3	doesn't see her children for many years.	☐	☐

CHAPTER FOUR
THE CLERK OF OXFORD'S TALE

he quiet Clerk looked sad when the Landlord said to him: 'Forget your books and your long face, and tell us a story. Remember, lots of interesting things must happen in it, and please make it easy for us to understand.'

'Very well,' answered the **poor** Clerk. 'It's an old Italian story, and – with God's help – we can all learn something from it about strong husbands and faithful wives.' Then he began:

✿

King Walter ruled Saluzzo in Italy. His people loved him, but he was sad because he had no wife and no son.

'I can only be happy with an **obedient** wife,' he said, but it wasn't easy to find an obedient woman in Saluzzo.

From time to time, King Walter went into town in dirty old clothes. He liked visiting his people when they didn't **recognize** him.

One day, in his old clothes, Walter met a poor man, Janicula, and his beautiful daughter – Griselda. Every day Griselda brought water home for her father, and Walter watched her at work. She was a good and obedient daughter. 'She's the **perfect** wife for me!' he **decided**.

So Walter – in his old clothes – visited Janicula.

'Can I marry your daughter?' he asked.

'Of course,' answered Janicula.

Then Walter spoke to Griselda. 'I want to marry you,' he said. 'I asked your father and he said "yes". But before we marry, promise me something.'

poor not rich; or something you say when you feel sorry for somone

obedient doing what people tell you to do

recognize to see someone and to know who it is

perfect with nothing wrong

decide to think about something and then do it

'What?' asked Griselda.

'When we are husband and wife, you must always be obedient. Sometimes it's going to hurt you, but you must never question me.'

'I promise,' said Griselda.

Then Walter said to Griselda, 'Now I can tell you my **secret**. I am King Walter!'

After the wedding, Griselda became famous in Saluzzo.

'What a good, beautiful woman!' people said. 'And what an obedient wife!'

Soon she had a daughter. When the child was very little, the king decided to **test** his wife.

'Our daughter can't stay with us,' he said. 'She must go and live in a house far away.'

Griselda remembered her promise before the wedding. 'Of course,' she said.

So Walter took their young daughter to a good family in a house far away, and left her there.

After two years, Griselda had a son. Everyone in Saluzzo was happy. But when the boy was two years old, Walter tested his wife again.

secret something that you don't tell to everybody

test to do something to someone to see what they do

23

'Our son can't stay with us,' he said. 'He must go and live in a house far away.'

Again Griselda remembered her promise before the wedding. 'Of course,' she said.

So Walter went back to the family in the house far away and left their young son there, with their daughter.

When their daughter was sixteen years old, and their son fourteen, the king decided to test Griselda one more time. He sat down at his writing-table and wrote a **false** letter. It said:

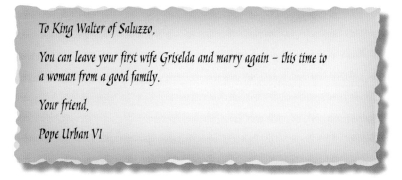

To King Walter of Saluzzo,

You can leave your first wife Griselda and marry again – this time to a woman from a good family.

Your friend,

Pope Urban VI

Walter took the false letter to Griselda and said, 'This is from the **Pope**. Now I can leave you and marry a rich young wife.'

Griselda felt very sad, but she remembered her promise. 'Of course,' she said. 'I can go back to live with my father.'

Then the king brought his son and his daughter back home in rich clothes. He didn't tell Griselda their true names, and – after twelve years away – she didn't recognize them.

'This is my new wife and her young brother,' said Walter.

false not true

Pope the most important man in the Catholic church; he lives in Rome

Then he asked Griselda, 'Before you leave, can you help my new wife into her wedding dress?'

'Of course,' she said, and she went to her daughter's room and helped the young girl into the beautiful dress.

After that, Griselda took off her rich queen's clothes, put on a poor woman's dress, and went back to her father's house.

'What a perfect wife!' said Walter.

At once, he took his children to Janicula's house. There he spoke to his wife.

'Griselda,' he said, 'the Pope's letter was false. There was no wedding today. I have no new wife. This is your daughter, Vera, and this is your son, Fidelio. I took them from you many years ago, but now they are back with us again.'

'Can this be true?' Griselda cried, with a smile on her face.

'Yes, mother, it's us,' said Vera and Fidelio.

At once, Griselda took her two children in her arms. All three of them cried happily.

Then they went back home with Walter. After that, the King stopped testing his wife, and they and their children lived happily in Saluzzo for many years.

READING CHECK

Match the sentence parts to tell the Clerk's story.

a King Walter is sad because	**1** to be obedient at all times.
b He wants to find	**2** the king brings his children home.
c Sometimes he wears old clothes	**3** an obedient wife.
d King Walter wants to marry Griselda because	**4** she is a good young woman.
e When they marry, Griselda promises	**5** he doesn't have a wife and children.
f After their daughter is born, King Walter	**6** never to test his wife again.
g The king takes their two children away	**7** wants to test his wife.
h When their daughter is sixteen	**8** and visits people in the town.
i Walter is going to marry a rich young woman,	**9** but his wife doesn't say a thing.
j In the end King Walter promises	**10** Griselda thinks.

WORD WORK

1 Put the letters on the books in order to make words from the Clerk's story.

a o<u>bedient</u>   **b** f_____   **c** d_____   **d** p_____

e p_____   **f** r_____   **g** s_____   **h** t_____

2 Complete Princess Vera's diary with the words from Activity 1 in the correct form.

October 12th

My mother was from a (a)..poor.. family before she married my father, the king. He visited her house every day but she didn't (b)...................... him in his old clothes. Sometimes he wore a (c)................ beard, too. He told her his (d)................ only after she promised to marry him.

My mother was a (e)................ wife, but my father wanted to (f)................ her. When they got married, she promised to be always (g)...................... and never to question him. When I was a small girl, my father (h)...................... to take me away from my mother. That was fourteen years ago! Tomorrow my father is going to take me and my brother home to our mother. We're very excited!

GUESS WHAT

The Merchant tells the next story. It has a rich old knight in it. What do you think the story is about? Tick four things.

a ☐ a bag of money

b ☐ a young woman

c ☐ a pear tree

d ☐ a small house

e ☐ a servant

f ☐ a goddess

CHAPTER FIVE

THE MERCHANT'S TALE

After the Clerk finished, the Merchant said: 'I married my wife two weeks ago, and she's not an obedient Griselda. She's a very bad young woman. She's always angry with me, and she never stops talking. I'm tired of it. For me, all wives are only punishments for their husbands.' He said no more about his wife after that, but began his story:

January was a rich old knight. He lived in the town of Pavia, in the north of Italy.

When he was younger, he had a good time. Now he was sixty, he wanted to marry a woman from his home town and have a son.

'My wife can help me when I'm very old and ill, and my son can have my house and everything in it when I die,' he thought.

In the end, January decided to marry a very young woman. Her name was May. Before the wedding, he asked his friends, 'Is she right for me?'

Most said, 'She's perfect!'

But his best friend, Justinius, said, 'It isn't good for an old man to marry a young girl. You're going to have **problems**.'

January didn't listen, and married May.

After the wedding dinner, he told his friends, 'Go now. I want to be **alone** with my young wife.'

They left at once, and January and May went to bed.

problem something that makes you feel bad

alone with nobody

Damian was a young **servant** in January's house. He fell in love with May when he first saw her. He soon became ill with this love – but told his secret to nobody.

'What's the matter with Damian?' January said to May. 'Wife, go and **look after** him.'

So May went and sat by Damian's bed.

Damian soon began to feel better. Once, when they were alone, he gave May a short letter. She read it:

> May,
> I love you a lot.
> Your servant,
> Damian

Then May looked up at Damian. 'I love you too,' she said.

Damian soon got out of bed after that.

Some time later, January suddenly became **blind**. He was now very **jealous** of May.

'Where are you? Stay next to me. Give me your hand,' he said. 'You must look after me.'

It wasn't easy for May. She wanted to be with Damian, but all the time her jealous old husband stopped her.

One morning at breakfast Damian quietly gave May a longer letter. January was there, but he couldn't see a

servant a person who works for someone rich

look after to do things for someone when they need help or are ill

blind when you can't see

jealous feeling angry or unhappy because someone you like is interested in someone else

thing. May said nothing, but she read Damian's letter at once. It said:

> May,
> Let's meet in the garden. I can go there before you, climb up into the **pear** tree, and wait for you. When you and January arrive, climb up into the tree, and we can kiss there.
> Damian
> XXX

'Shall we go for a walk in the garden?' May asked January after breakfast.

'Yes,' he answered. He took May's hand blindly, and walked with her into the garden.

At the same time, in the country of the dead, the god Pluto – King of Hades – spoke to his wife, Queen Proserpina.

'I'm angry with May,' said Pluto. 'She's not faithful to January. Poor blind January. I'm going to help him. He's going to see again. That's going to stop May.'

'I'm not sorry for January,' said Proserpina. 'He's a **foolish** old man. He married a young girl for her face and body, and didn't see any problem in that. I'm going to help May. When January sees his young wife in the tree with Damian, she's going to be ready with a quick answer for her husband.'

Back in Italy, May and January sat under the pear tree in the garden. Damian waited up in the tree.

pear a long green or yellow fruit with a round bottom

foolish not thinking well

'Husband, are you hungry?' asked May.

'Yes,' said January.

'Would you like a nice pear from the tree?' asked May.

'Yes.'

So May climbed up into the tree. Quietly Damian began kissing and **hugging** her.

Just then, January could suddenly see again. He looked up and saw Damian and May.

'What are you doing?' he said. 'I can see you. You're hugging and kissing Damian!' cried January angrily.

'What are you talking about?' said May. 'Yesterday an old woman told me, "Fight with a man in a pear tree, and your blind husband is going to see again." Damian fought with me in the tree because I asked him. And you can see again, so it worked! So don't be angry with me. Say "thank you".'

'Perhaps you're right.' said January, 'I can see now because you fought with Damian in the pear tree. Thank you, wife, for that.'

May climbed quickly down from the tree. She smiled up at Damian, hugged January, and took her foolish old husband back into the house.

hug to take lovingly in your arms

ACTIVITIES

READING CHECK

1 Are these sentences true or false?

		True	False
a	January marries for love.	☐	☑
b	Damian works in January's house.	☐	☐
c	Damian becomes ill because of his love for May.	☐	☐
d	May looks after Damian in secret.	☐	☐
e	May writes a love letter to Damian.	☐	☐
f	Damian and May decide to meet in the garden.	☐	☐
g	The gods Pluto and Proserpina help May and Damian.	☐	☐
h	January sees May and Damian kissing in a tree.	☐	☐
i	In the end January is angry with May.	☐	☐

2 Who says what? Match the speech bubbles with the people.

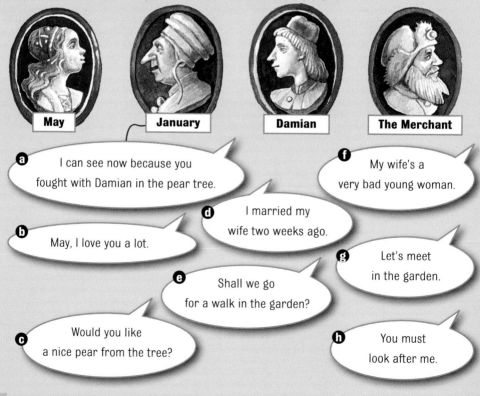

May **January** **Damian** **The Merchant**

a I can see now because you fought with Damian in the pear tree.

f My wife's a very bad young woman.

d I married my wife two weeks ago.

b May, I love you a lot.

g Let's meet in the garden.

e Shall we go for a walk in the garden?

c Would you like a nice pear from the tree?

h You must look after me.

WORD WORK

Replace the yellow words with words from the Merchant's story.

a Damian and May kiss in a bear tree. ......*pear*......

b January is jeans of May. He doesn't like it when men look at her. ....

c January needs May's help because he's find and can't see. ....

d January sees May and Damian kissing and hungry in the tree. ....

e Old January was finish to marry young May, thinks Proserpina. ....

f January has lots of programs with his wife. ....

g Damian is a serpent in January's house. ....

h It isn't easy for May to be along with Damian because she likes him. ....

GUESS WHAT

The Franklin tells the last story. Complete the sentences with the names.

a .... is a good knight.

b .... and .... are married.

c .... falls in love with ....

d .... is faithful and doesn't love ....

Arveragus

Dorigen

Aurelius

CHAPTER SIX
THE FRANKLIN'S TALE

Before the Franklin began his story, he said: 'I never learnt much from books because I didn't go to a good school. My story's about a husband and wife, too. But – for me – when a man and woman marry, the two of them must rule in their home – differently, of course – for it to be a happy one.' And, with that, he began:

Arveragus was a good, rich knight. He lived in a castle on a black hill near the sea in Brittany in France. One day he decided to marry.

He chose for his wife a beautiful young woman, Dorigen. Before the wedding he said to her, 'When we are husband and wife, I'm always going to think well of you, and I'm never going to be angry when you say or do foolish things. Can you promise me this, too?'

'Of course,' said Dorigen, and she promised.

Soon after the wedding, Arveragus went away to a different country. Dorigen felt **lonely**. She often went down to watch the sea. It hit the black **rocks** for hours. Dorigen watched it sadly, and waited for her husband to come home.

A rich man, Aurelius, lived near Arveragus's castle. Day after day he saw Dorigen from his window, and he fell in love with her. He began to go for walks by the sea. One day he spoke to Dorigen.

'Would you like to come to my castle for dinner?'

'I'm sorry,' said the faithful Dorigen, 'I can't. I'm waiting for my husband.'

lonely unhappy because you are alone

rock a very big stone

Day after day Dorigen watched the sea. Day after day Aurelius came and spoke to her.

'Would you like a drink?'

'Would you like to meet my friends?'

Always Dorigen's answer was, 'No.'

But one morning in May, Aurelius said, 'Dorigen, would you like to come on a **picnic**?'

And this time Dorigen said, 'Yes.'

Aurelius ran home at once. He put lots of good things to eat in a picnic box, took it back to Dorigen, and opened it. He gave a red apple to Dorigen. She sat on a little rock near him, and ate it.

Soon Aurelius said, 'Dorigen, I love you. Your husband's away. You can come to my castle in secret. I want you.'

'No,' she said.

'Dorigen, think again. You're alone. Come to my castle. I need you.'

Dorigen laughed. 'Aurelius, I promise you something. First take away all the rocks from the sea near Brittany. Then you and I can meet in your castle,' she **joked**.

picnic a meal that people eat outside in the country, often sitting on the ground

joke to say things that are not serious, or are funny

After the picnic, Aurelius went home to his castle, and Dorigen stayed and watched the sea.

🎵

One day, Arveragus came home after many months. He and Dorigen hugged and kissed when they met.

'I'm happy to be back,' he said.

'I'm happy to have you here again,' said Dorigen.

🎵

But on that day – at the same time – Aurelius met a **magician**. He told the man about Dorigen's promise.

'For £1,000 I can take away all the rocks from the sea near Brittany,' the magician said.

'Do it, and I can give you the money the day after tomorrow,' said Aurelius.

🎵

Early the next morning the rocks weren't there. Aurelius came at once to see Dorigen.

'Remember your promise. I'm waiting for you tonight,' he said. Then he went back to his castle.

Dorigen remembered her foolish joke and felt sad.

'What's the matter?' asked Arveragus at breakfast.

magician
somebody that makes things happen in a way that you don't understand

Dorigen told him all about the picnic and her foolish promise.

Arveragus said, 'Dorigen, I'm sorry. It was a joke, I know, but a promise is a promise. It's going to hurt me a lot, but there are no rocks in the sea today. So you must go to Aurelius tonight.'

ᕽ

Aurelius smiled when he opened his door to Dorigen that night. But then he saw her sad face. 'What did your husband say?' he asked.

When Dorigen told him, Aurelius said, 'Your husband's a very good man, and I feel very bad. A joke's a joke after all. Look, I'm going to bed, and you must go back to Arveragus!'

So Dorigen went home to her husband.

The next day, the magician visited Aurelius.

'Where's my money?' he said. 'And what happened with Dorigen?'

Aurelius told him about the night before.

'You poor man!' said the magician. 'After all that, you didn't get the girl. Well, Arveragus is a good husband, Dorigen's a good wife, and I'm a good magician. So let's forget the £1,000.'

'Thank you very much, my friend,' said Aurelius.

ᕽ

In the end, after all these interesting stories and more – we **pilgrims** arrived in Canterbury. There we visited Saint Thomas's tomb and said our 'thank yous' to God. But things didn't finish there, because we told lots more stories on the road back from Canterbury, too.

pilgrim a person who visits a holy place

READING CHECK

Correct ten more mistakes in the summary of the Franklin's story.

Before Arveragus marries Dorigen, they make a promise never to be ~~happy~~ angry. When Arveragus goes away to a different city, Dorigen is sad. She sits and watches the sky, waiting for her husband to come home.

Aurelius is a poor man and he falls in love with Dorigen. He asks her to his garden, but she never goes with him. One day they go on a ship. There Dorigen promises to visit Aurelius after he takes away all the water from the sea. Aurelius meets a magician and asks for his help.

Arveragus comes home, but Dorigen is only happy for a short time. The next day there are no ships in the sea. She tells her husband about her promise. 'You mustn't go to Aurelius,' he says. When Dorigen tells Aurelius about her husband, he feels bad. 'Go to my bed,' he tells her. Then Aurelius tells the story to the magician, and the magician takes money from Aurelius for his help.

WORD WORK

Complete the sentences on page 39 with words from the sea.

joke   ~~magician~~   rocks

lonely   picnic

a The .magician. took some interesting things out of his hat.

b They had a nice .... with lots of good things to eat in the country.

c He felt .... without his wife and children.

d His .... wasn't very good but she laughed at it.

e The ship hit some .... and began to go down.

GUESS WHAT

There are many more Canterbury Tales. Match the summaries with the pictures.

a Constance has lots of problems, but she's always OK in the end. ☐

b Two students from Oxford play jokes on a bad miller. ☐

c Some bad people kill a young boy after he sings a song. ☐

d A student falls in love with the wife of a foolish man. ☐

e A hen's husband tells people about bad things that are going to happen. ☐

The Prioress's Story

The Monk's Story

The Lawyer's Story

The Miller's Story

The Reeve's Story

Project A — *Planning a film*

1 Read a character card for a
film of *The Knight's Tale*.

Which character is it for?

Name: _____
age: 19 or 20
build: tall, thin
looks: fair hair, beautiful
character: nice, friendly

Notes:
Hippolyta's sister
Arcite and Palamon are in love with her
marries Palamon in the end

2 Complete the character card
for Palamon.

Name: Palamon
age: early 20s
build: _____ , _____
looks: _____ , _____
character: _____ , _____

Notes:
good _____
Arcite's _____
becomes Theseus's _____

3 Make cards for the other main characters
in the story.

Name: Theseus
age: _____
build: _____ , _____
looks: _____ , _____
character: _____ , _____

Notes:
_____
_____
_____

Name: Hippolyta
age: _____
build: _____ , _____
looks: _____ , _____
character: _____ , _____

Notes:
_____
_____
_____

Name: Arcite
age: _____
build: _____ , _____
looks: _____ , _____
character: _____ , _____

Notes:
_____
_____
_____

4 You want to make a film of *The Knight's Tale*.
Decide which actors and actresses are going to
play the main characters. Compare your ideas.

5 Choose a different Canterbury Tale. Make cards
for the main characters. Choose actors
and actresses to be in the film.

Project B *Describing a holy place*

1 Read the texts below and match the events with the dates on page 43.

Canterbury Cathedral

The Cathedral at Canterbury is a famous holy place in Britain. Canterbury was an important city in Roman times because it was on the road from London to Rome. In the year 597 Saint Augustine arrived in Canterbury from Rome. He started the first Christian church in England there. The building of the cathedral began in 1070, but there was a terrible fire in 1174 and it burnt down.

Tomb of Thomas Becket

In 1170 four of the King of England's knights killed the Archbishop Thomas Becket in the cathedral. Thousands of medieval travellers visited his tomb. Chaucer's travellers in *The Canterbury Tales* (1386-1400) were some of them.

Canterbury Cathedral is the largest medieval church in Europe. The oldest part, Trinity Chapel, dates from 1175.

The Black Prince

The tomb of The Black Prince – son of Edward III – is here. He died in 1376.

Today Canterbury is an important sight for tourists from all round the world. The cathedral is famous for its stained glass windows. The oldest – a picture of Adam – dates from 1176.

Dates		Events
500AD		
a 597		**1** Building of Trinity Chapel
b 1070		**2** People begin travelling to the cathedral
		3 The cathedral burns down
c 1170		**4** Building of the first cathedral begins
d 1174		**5** Thomas Becket dies in the cathedral
e 1175		
f 1176		**6** Chaucer begins writing The Canterbury Tales
		7 Saint Augustine starts a Christian church in Canterbury
		8 First stained glass window
g 1376		**9** The Black Prince dies
h 1386		
1400		

2 Use the notes to complete the text about the Alhambra on page 44.

Place: *The Alhambra*

Description: large, beautiful palace – gardens, fountains and courtyards

Importance: once main Islamic centre in Europe; home of Muslim kings for more than two hundred years

Geography: in Granada, south eastern Spain, on hill next to River Darro

History

1248 – 1354 Building of Alhambra by Muslim king Mohammed Ibn Al-Ahmar

1492 Christian kings – Ferdinand and Isabella – take Granada from Muslim king

1516-1556 Charles V makes many changes to buildings

1700-1746 Philip V builds Italian palace

1812 Napoleon nearly destroys Alhambra

1821 Earthquake hits many buildings

1828 Rebuilding work starts

1832 Washington Irving writes 'Tales of the Alhambra' in Granada

The beautiful courtyard of the Lions

The Alhambra

The Alhambra in .... in .... is a
beautiful .... It was the .... centre in Europe,
and the home of Muslim .... for over .... years.

King .... started the palace in ....
Building finished in 1354. The palace had green .... with lots of noisy
.... in them, beautiful open .... , and a mosque.

In 1492 the .... Ferdinand and Isabella took Granada and the
Alhambra from the .... king, Boabdil.

.... (1516 – 1556) made a lot of .... to the Alhambra buildings.
Later Philip V (1700 – 1746) built an .... there. In 1812
.... nearly destroyed it and in .... an earthquake hit many of the
buildings. Work to rebuild the Alhambra began in ....

.... wrote '................. of the ....' in Granada
in 1832. Many people were interested in the palace after they read the book.

Now more than 8,000 people from all round the world visit the Alhambra every day.

3 Find out about one of these places, or a holy place in your country. Write notes.

Place	Description	Importance	Geography	History

Mecca, Saudi Arabia

Machu Picchu, Peru

The Golden Temple, Amritsar, India

4 Use your notes to write about your holy place.

GRAMMAR CHECK

Present Continuous

We use the Present Continuous to talk about things happening now.

We make the Present Continuous with the verb be + the –ing form of the verb.

The Clerk's wearing dark blue.

When short verbs end in consonant + vowel + consonant, we double the final consonant and add –ing.

begin – The Wife of Bath's face is beginning to go red.

When verbs end in consonant + –e, we remove the e and add –ing.

take – The Merchant is taking his time over breakfast.

We put n't (not) with the verb be to make the Present Continuous negative.

The landlord isn't sitting. The pilgrims aren't standing.

1 **Complete the text about the Canterbury pilgrims with the Present Continuous form of the verbs in brackets.**

In this picture five pilgrims a) .*are sitting*. (sit) at the table in the Inn in Southwark. They b).............. (have) something to eat and drink. The Wife of Bath c).............. (talk) to the Franklin. She d).............. (put) up her hand and she e).............. (smile). She f).............. (wear) a hat, and a red dress. The Franklin g).............. (move) nearer to her, and he h).............. (laugh). The landlord i).............. (stand) in front of the table. He j).............. (give) the Merchant something to drink. The Knight and the Clerk k).............. (look) down. They l).............. (not smile). The Clerk m).............. (read) a book. A knife n).............. (sit) on the table in front of him. A little dog o).............. (watch) the pilgrims hungrily.

GRAMMAR CHECK

Going to Future

We make the *going to* future with the verb be + going to + the infinitive form.

We can use the *going to* future to talk about plans and intentions.

I'm going to be famous.

We can also use the *going to* future to make predictions.

They aren't going to win the war.

2 **Imagine it is the night before the big fight in *The Knight's Tale*. Write predictions with these words in the *going to* future.**

a Arcite / win / the fight ....*Arcite's going to win the fight.*....

b People / cry / Arcite's name ....

c Arcite's horse / be / afraid ....

d It / stand / on its back legs ....

e Arcite / fall / from his horse ....

f He / die ....

g He / not / marry Emely ....

h He / be / very famous ....

i Palamon and Emely / marry ....

j They / live / in Thebes ....

k They / have / lots of children ....

l They / not be / poor ....

GRAMMAR CHECK

Past Simple: Yes/No questions and short answers

We use auxiliary verbs and be (main verb) in Yes/No questions.

Did the Wife of Bath have five husbands?

Was she happy with her poor young husbands?

In the short answer we re-use the auxiliary verb and be (main verb).

Yes, she did.

No, she wasn't. (was not)

3 **Do you remember *The Wife of Bath's Tale*? Write short answers for the questions about the story.**

a Was Tarquin one of King Arthur's knights? Yes, he was.

b Was he a good knight? ....

c Did he treat Lucretia badly? ....

d Did he kill her? ....

e Did the knights of Camelot come to Arthur when he called them? ....

f Could they find Tarquin quickly? ....

g Did they kill Tarquin? ....

h Was Arthur angry with Tarquin? ....

i Did Guinevere say to Arthur, 'Tarquin must die!'? ....

j Did Guinevere ask Tarquin a question?

....

k Could Tarquin answer her question at once?

....

l Could he answer it after a year?

....

m Were the young women in the forest ugly?

....

n Was the old woman in the forest beautiful?

....

o Were Tarquin and his wife happy in the end?

....

GRAMMAR

GRAMMAR CHECK

Past Simple: questions

In Past Simple questions most verbs take did + subject + the infinitive without *to*.

Where did King Walter live? Saluzzo.

What did his people think of him? They loved him.

The verbs be and can are different. With them, we put the subject after the past verb to make past questions.

Why was he sad? Because he had no wife.

Where could he find a wife? In town.

4 Do you remember *The Clerk of Oxford's Tale*? Write Past Simple questions for the answers about the story. Use the words in brackets.

a ...How did King Walter go into town?... In dirty old clothes.

(how / King Walter / go into town)

b .... So his people couldn't recognize him.

(why / he / wear / these)

c .... Always to be obedient.

(what / Griselda / promise Walter)

d .... Two.

(how many children / they / have)

e .... Vera and Fidelio.

(what / be / their names)

f .... To a house far away.

(where / Walter / take / them)

g .... When Vera was 16, and Fidelio was 14.

(when / be / Walter's last test of Griselda)

h .... His 'new wife' and her brother.

(who / he / bring / home)

i .... 'These are your children.'

(what / Walter / say / to Griselda)

j .... Walter stopped testing Griselda.

(how / the story / end)

48

GRAMMAR CHECK

Past Simple: affirmative

With regular verbs we usually add –d/–ed to the infinitive without *to*.

The Merchant loved money. He talked about ships and the sea a lot.

With regular verbs that end in consonant + –y we change y to i and add –ed.

marry – He married a young wife.

Some verbs are irregular. You must learn their past forms.

wear – He wore rich red and yellow clothes.

January   May   Damian

5   **Do you remember *The Merchant's Tale*? Complete the text about the story with the Past Simple form of the verbs in brackets.**

January a) ....was.... (be) a rich old man. He b) .... (live) in Pavia. He c) .... (marry) a young woman. He d) .... (choose) May, a very young woman for his wife. Damian e) .... (work) for January. He f) .... (fall) in love with May when he g) .... (see) her, and he soon h) .... (feel) ill because of it. May i) .... (go) and j) .... (visit) him. He k) .... (give) her a short love letter and she l) .... (read) it. May and Damian m) .... (be) soon in love. At about that time, January n) .... (become) blind and very jealous. May cannot do a thing without him. But she and Damian o) .... (want) to kiss and hug. So one day Damian p) .... (wait) in a pear tree in the garden. Later May q) .... (climb) up into the tree, too, for some pears for January. Then suddenly – because the god Pluto r) .... (help) him – January s) .... (can) see again, and he t) .... (see) his young wife up in the tree in Damian's arms. But with some help from the goddess Proserpina, May u) .... (have) a quick answer ready for him.

GRAMMAR CHECK

Time clauses with before, after, and when

before links a later action with an earlier action.

Before Dorigen married Arveragus, she promised always to think well of him.

Dorigen promised always to think well of Arveragus before she married him.

after links an earlier action with a later action.

After they married, Arveragus went away.

Arveragus went away after they married.

when links two actions close in time, where the first action is the reason for the second action.

When Dorigen felt sad, she went down to the sea.

Dorigen went down to the sea when she felt sad.

Dorigen

We can put *before*, *after* and *when* clauses at the start of the sentence or at the end.

When we write the time clause first, we must use a comma.

6 Do you remember *The Franklin's Tale*? Complete the sentences with *before*, *after*, or *when*.

a Aurelius fell in love with Dorigen ...after... he saw her from his window.

b Aurelius went for a number of walks by the sea .... he spoke to Dorigen.

c .... he asked Dorigen to a picnic, she said 'yes'.

d Aurelius went to see a magician .... Dorigen joked about taking the rocks away from the sea.

e Arveragus and Dorigen hugged and kissed .... Arveragus came back home.

f .... Arveragus came home, the rocks went from the sea.

g .... Dorigen had breakfast with her husband, Aurelius came to see her.

h .... Dorigen told her husband about her foolish promise, Arveragus said, 'You must go to Aurelius!'

i Aurelius had a smile on his face .... he saw Dorigen's sad face.

j .... Dorigen told Aurelius about her husband, Aurelius felt bad.

k Dorigen went home .... Arveragus said, 'I'm going to bed!'

l .... the magician visited Aurelius the next day, he asked for his money.

m The magician said, 'Let's forget it!' .... he heard Aurelius's story.

Past Simple: negative

In the Past Simple negative we use didn't (did not) + infinitive without *to*.

Chaucer didn't watch TV.

The verb be has two past negative forms – wasn't (was not) and weren't (were not).

Chaucer wasn't famous in those days. (singular)

His stories weren't on the radio. (plural)

7 Some of these sentences about England in Chaucer's time are false. Correct them.

a People drove cars. .... *People didn't drive cars.* ....

b People ate hamburgers. ....

c People had telephones. ....

d People saw films at the cinema. ....

e People wore hats. ....

f People took photos with cameras. ....

g People drank cola. ....

h People rode horses. ....

i There were lots of supermarkets. ....

j England was very expensive. ....

k People went to different countries by plane. ....

DOMINOES
THE STRUCTURED APPROACH TO READING IN ENGLISH

Dominoes is an enjoyable series of illustrated classic and modern stories in four carefully graded language stages – from Starter to Three – which take learners from beginner to intermediate level.

Each *Domino* reader includes:
- **a good story** to read and enjoy
- **integrated activities** to develop reading skills and increase active vocabulary
- **personalized projects** to make the language and story themes more meaningful
- **seven pages of grammar activities** for consolidation.

Each *Domino* pack contains a reader, plus a MultiROM with:
- **a complete audio recording of the story**, fully dramatized to bring it to life
- **interactive activities** to offer further practice in reading and language skills and to consolidate learning.

If you liked this Level One *Domino*, why not read these?

Macbeth
William Shakespeare

A dark, rainy day in Scotland, long ago. Returning from battle, Macbeth and his friend Banquo meet three witches. 'Macbeth, the king!' they say, but Macbeth is not a king, he is just a simple soldier.

Macbeth and Banquo cannot forget the witches' words. Soon Macbeth is king, but his wife walks in her sleep at night, and dreams of blood. What lies in the future for Banquo? And how many people must die before Scotland finds peace once more?

Book ISBN: 978 0 19 424756 6
MultiROM Pack ISBN: 978 0 19 424720 7

The Wrong Trousers™
Aardman

It's Gromit the dog's birthday, and his friend Wallace gives him an unusual present – a pair of techno-trousers.

At first Wallace uses the trousers to take Gromit for walks, but when the penguin comes to stay, he uses them one night for something different – very different.

This strange story won the Oscar® for Best Animated Short Film in 1990.

Book ISBN: 978 0 19 424757 3
MultiROM Pack ISBN: 978 0 19 424721 4

You can find details and a full list of books in the *Dominoes* catalogue and Oxford English Language Teaching Catalogue, and on the website: www.oup.com/elt

Teachers: see www.oup.com/elt for a full range of online support, or consult your local office.

	CEFR	Cambridge Exams	IELTS	TOEFL iBT	TOEIC
Level 3	B1	PET	4.0	57-86	550
Level 2	A2–B1	KET-PET	3.0-4.0	–	–
Level 1	A1–A2	YLE Flyers/KET	3.0	–	–
Starter & Quick Starter	A1	YLE Movers	–	–	–